A Poetry Lover's Poetry Collection

Karley Lamb

BookLeaf Publishing

India | USA | UK

Presentation by *BookLeaf Publishing*

Web: www.bookleafpub.com

E-mail: info@bookleafpub.com

ISBN: 978-93-5744-981-6

First edition 2022

DEDICATION

This book is dedicated to Ms. Lisco and Kristen for making me a better writer, and to my parents for giving me an exciting world to write about.

ACKNOWLEDGEMENT

Thank you to all of my editors, supporters, sources of inspiration and fellow writers who helped my mind find the right words to express myself.

Clouds

We found beaches in the clouds
Driving towards the beaches
On a country road, windows-down drive

The clouds have pink shadows
In the pink of the setting sun
After hiding away from the blue sky expanse

Your dreams love among the clouds
And you shoot for the stars
That we made love under

Street Lit Treasures

She loved the small that followed a storm
After the rain had sobbed all day long
Leaving a refreshed mess under the yellow
streetlights

She loved to walk where sadness had struck
Exploring the streets in treasured two a.m.
solitude
When even the rain clouds had gone to sleep

She loved to listen to covert crickets under a
starlit sky
As she greeted the awakening suburban nightlife
To a clear black atmosphere

Red Autumn

Fall crimson leaf
Treasured, autumn breeze severs
Marble bench landing

Softly Treasured

White cotton balls stuck to a pastel blue sky
Lovely atmosphere holds the sun up high
Graceful birds floating above
Tree branches tickle the blue roof with love

A gentle breeze blows
Through the peaceful meadow
Starting the green grass' spring dance
As if each thin strand was captured in a trance

Trees calmly sway
Dandelion fluff is blown away
Caressing velvet flower petals
Before the breeze lets the sweet meadow dance
settle

Pale asters colour the scene
Soft flower beds feel serene
Pretty pinks mixed with intense indigos
Glowing amber beside my toes

Splotches of colour sitting upon a rippling sea of
green
A secret treasure; its reveal unforeseen
This tranquil valley that I have found

Is to me a most cherished ground

The Treasure Within

Each wooden wall,
Sheltering the secrets of the library
Creating an escape from the outside world,
Buzzing with hushed energy,
Lit by the dim glow of old lanterns,
Crowded by piles of books that don't have a
place on the shelves,
Hiding every last inch of wall space in the room

Each shelf is bending with weight and
knowledge,
Crammed with hundreds of books,
Loaded with thousands of stories,
Sitting patiently on wooden planks,
Waiting to be chosen,
Stirring the dust that has settled
On the sturdy shelves around bounded books

Each book is an enchanting world,
Brought to life from one person's imagination,
Compressed into a beginning, middle and end,
Sitting between other books, both similar and
different from itself,
Wrapped with its own unique sleeve

Hinting at the true treasure of a book;
The content that is captured within

Each page, whether old or new
Holds a life that was scribbled there
And will be turned to reveal the next,
Imprinted with letters
String together to make words,
Arranged carefully to make phrases,
Joined to tell the dreamiest stories of far away
lands and adventures we will only have while
reading

A Dwindling Treasure

Whispering wind
Rustling leaves
Sunlight peeking through the trees

Hanging pine needles
Damp, hushed sounds
Pinecones resting on the ground

Rows of trunks
Standing tall
Putting up a protective wall

A cave of wonders
Hidden within its boundaries
A tranquil escape, solely for me

Treasured land
Becoming bare
This life will soon be lost
All because we do not care

Tiny Treasures

A warm breeze blows freely,
Waves crash down,
The sun shines brightly in the afternoon sky,
A turquoise ocean reaches for the horizon,
Palm trees stand tall,
The white sand rises between my toes,
A sailboat glides across the water,
As I enjoy my hidden paradise,
My piece of the sea,
Where many treasures and brought to me
By the cool blue tide.
Sand dollars, sea glass and shells
Often adorn the soaked shoreline,
Yet I am always entranced by their beauty
For items so fragile
Tossed in and out by the deep
Have strength and stories behind them

Treasured Night

A magnificent chandelier sparkles like a crown
Elegant red curtains frame the grand, glass door
A golden staircase leading down
To the royal ballroom with a marble floor

Romantic music floats through the air,
The King and Queen rise from their thrones,
To take their place as the first pair
And dance to joyous resounding tones

Beautiful ball gowns glimmer
As princes lead fair maidens in dance.
The castle's energy surpassing a simmer
For this magic fairytale chance

But nothing lasts forever
Sooner or later they will see
And this marvellous dream-come-true
Will become nothing but a treasured memory

Abandoned Treasure

Bare branches scratch grey skies
Lifeless bullrushes line a grey river
The faded wood of aa surviving dock
Once a treasure, but now abandoned

Shadow's persistent presence under grey clouds
Bitter wind chills the air
Thick mist dampens the barren ground
Once a treasure, but now abandoned

A lonely lakeside
A melancholy margin
A solitary strand
Once a treasure, but now abandoned

Celestial Canvas

A purple moon floats in the sky
Demanding the eye's attention
To its cutting earthly swirls
But the sky behind
is not a dark starry night;
It is alive with nature's spirits

Cosmic pink and violet mist
Fill the buzzing atmosphere
Before fading into a warm, orange forest

A cerulean canopy
Streaked with teal trees
And tall mauve stones
The ground littered with fallen blue leaves

A mirror of our world
With brighter colours
It is celestial, yet earthly
A spiritual representation of Earth

Raised scratches decorate the forest
Bringing it to life within its frame
The moon's edges are pinched with time
Layers of timeless life captured in this Rising
Round

Reasons to Work

I'm here to teach
I'm here to preach
I'm here 'cause I was told to get off my seat

We want to make a difference
We want to do what we love
We want food to eat and to stay off the street

We love the kids
We value quality
We're just here to pick up a cheque

Day in, day out
fools trick themselves
to be happy with this forced routine

Little Sister

Built to withstand a hurricane,
Strong and earthly beautiful
Too innocent to realize the magnitude of her
strength

She speaks in colourful bubbles of emotion,
Laughter and uncontainable smiles swirl around
her
Warm brown eyes actually sparkle when she
laughs pure joy

Yet there are days she is a thicket of thorns
Rooted deep down and unmoveable
Only time will allow the thorns to leave

Some days, the storm blows inside her heart,
Her heart that is still pure
Has not learned this stubbornness

I hope it never does

My Flower Shop

Some people come in knowing exactly what
they need:
Red roses please.
A bouquet of daisies; they're her favourite,
he tells me with a smile.
Snipped stems and removed thorns
lay scattered on the desk as the door chimes
goodbye

Others guess hoping not to pick the wrong one,
Knowing less about the differences between one
type and another:
She said her dress is burgundy… Do you have
something that will match that?
Something pink and pretty, maybe that bouquet
behind you,
She says pointing to one of the fridges behind
the counter.
Pretty paper crinkles as its wrapped protectively
around the pink

Some people know an awful lot
for not working in a flower shop:
I'd like to get a pot of peonies please,
And could I get a card to go with it?

She chooses a simple card and holder
I match strands of ribbons to her flower and card
colours

Afternoon sunshine!
Sounds my week's end.
A kind, old man routinely visits
Purchasing a mixed bouquet of his colour of
choosing
Greens this week, please.
He says as I lean the broom against the counter

real-life tragedy, a blackout poem

human tragedy
creation imaginatively deranged
lover shaping history
spiralled ballroom
abyss triggers discomfort
depth has unhinged a heart
interpretation flaws character
backdrop of horrors result

Small centimetres

Walking on the ground, but far from grounded
Mind a million miles away
Brain coming in and out of focus
Not wanting to be part of today

Eyes focusing in and out
make the asphalt look as if it breathes
like a chest rising and falling
with ragged breaths and tears

Puffy with pain
and irritated red
from trying to cry away the sadness
Blinking her tears down already damp cheeks

Rubbing at agitated eyes
so she could continue staring
Small centimetres scattered on skin
Raised white tally marks
and new irritated red, no longer just in her eyes

The Colour Blue

A clear sky
A deep sea
The colour of his eyes
The pale shade of nail polish
that delicately covers her toes

A bright addicting screen
A sign of his new life
A dark mistake of a bruise
A low feeling that is both
overwhelmingly heartbreaking and numbing in
the same moment

A faded pair of jeans
An old living room carpet.
That old, patterned, fleece blanket
A vision you can't quite place in time
as a smell pokes at your memory

The colour blue is her favourite,
but what does it make her think of?
Where does her mind go when she sees blue,
cerulean,
navy,
cobalt,

teal.
Where does blue take her heart to make it soar
in the wondrous blue sky above

she wanted

She wanted to live by the water.
A simple life with a complex mind.
A cozy library with a window seat
to hear thunderstorms
and bathe in the sun.
A big porch to sip tea on
in rocking chairs and porch swings,
peace and subtle awe surrounding her.
And a beautiful sky full of stars
to fall in love under,
to celebrate and wonder and imagine about life
with the company of the awakened sky

Rose gold and opal

Rose gold rings and rose gold hair
Sapphire eyes and an opal stone
Freckled skin and a speckled past
Scarred hands and a scar of a story

Love Haikus

Flirty winks and grins
Shy smiling, batted lashes
Teenage lovers fall

Lips touch fleshy lips
Lashes flutter and hearts fall
Into reckless hands

A thank you poem

I remember her perfume

She recognizes me by last name on day one,
excited for the semester and to have me.
Great expectations as we begin with Great
Expectations

Sweet and harsh all at once.
Kind, loving, mothering heart
and direct, no-nonsense, red pen feedback.

A good idea, but say what you mean.
A paragraph reduced to three acceptable words.

I returned to her
to better my pen
Challenged on paper,
but challenged in mind that year too

She called me a shining light
She gave me passion and an escape

My student desk beside her computer desk
Her perfume would find me as she worked.
Even more memorable - as if she needed to be

Daisies

Innocent daisies
Sway lovely with summer's breeze
Simple love of mine